Doe

AKRON SERIES IN POETRY

AKRON SERIES IN POETRY
Mary Biddinger, Editor

Aimée Baker, *Doe*
Emily Rosko, *Weather Inventions*
Emilia Phillips, *Empty Clip*
Anne Barngrover, *Brazen Creature*
Matthew Guenette, *Vasectomania*
Sandra Simonds, *Further Problems with Pleasure*
Leslie Harrison, *The Book of Endings*
Emilia Phillips, *Groundspeed*
Philip Metres, *Pictures at an Exhibition: A Petersburg Album*
Jennifer Moore, *The Veronica Maneuver*
Brittany Cavallaro, *Girl-King*
Oliver de la Paz, *Post Subject: A Fable*
John Repp, *Fat Jersey Blues*
Emilia Phillips, *Signaletics*
Seth Abramson, *Thievery*
Steve Kistulentz, *Little Black Daydream*
Jason Bredle, *Carnival*
Emily Rosko, *Prop Rockery*
Alison Pelegrin, *Hurricane Party*
Matthew Guenette, *American Busboy*
Joshua Harmon, *Le Spleen de Poughkeepsie*

Titles published since 2010.
For a complete listing of titles published in the series,
go to www.uakron.edu/uapress/poetry.

Doe

Aimée Baker

The University of Akron Press
Akron, Ohio

Copyright © 2018 by The University of Akron Press
All rights reserved • First Edition 2018 • Manufactured in the United States of America.
All inquiries and permission requests should be addressed to the publisher,
The University of Akron Press, Akron, Ohio 44325-1703.

ISBN: 978-1-629220-84-0 (paper)
ISBN: 978-1-629220-85-7 (ePDF)
ISBN: 978-1-629220-86-4 (ePub)

Library of Congress Cataloging-in-Publication Data
Names: Baker, Aimée, author.
Title: Doe / Aimée Baker.
Description: Akron, Ohio : The University of Akron Press, [2018] | Series: Akron series
in poetry | Includes bibliographical references. | Identifiers: LCCN 2017051216 (print)
| LCCN 2018000080 (ebook) | ISBN 9781629220857 (ePDF) | ISBN 9781629220864
(ePub) | ISBN 9781629220840 (pbk. : alk. paper)
Classification: LCC PS3602.A5835 (ebook) | LCC PS3602.A5835 A6 2018 (print) |
DDC 811/.6—dc23
LC record available at https://lccn.loc.gov/2017051216

∞The paper used in this publication meets the minimum requirements of ANSI/NISO
Z39.48–1992 (Permanence of Paper).

Cover image: *Dream* by Max Wanger. Cover design by Amy Freels.

Doe was designed and typeset in Minion by Amy Freels and printed on sixty-pound
natural and bound by Bookmasters of Ashland, Ohio.

Contents

MISSING

The Abduction Narrative   3

Conductance   5

Cynosure   6

Surrender, Dorothy   7

Dustland Fairytale   9

Madrigal of the Sierra Nevadas   10

Scorpiris   11

Backland   14

Bloom   15

In the Midst of a Divorce   17

What the Eye Can't See   19

Ornithology   20

This is what the heart sounds like   22

The Fox Twin Theaters Plays *The Omen*   23

Light/Dark   24

Rubicon   25

The Body in Motion   27

The Origin of Language   28

Inamorato   30

How the Ocean and the Desert Meet   31

Stridulation   32

After the Maison de Mere   33

The Reading of the Fates of Love and Death   34

Rest Your Head Beside the Mountains   35

The Saints of the Last Days   36

UNIDENTIFIED

In the cursed country   51

Detroit, and Other Sorrows   52

The Killing Field   54

Our Bodies, the Ocean   55
Underbrush   56
Prime   58
Fourteen Pounds   59
Victim #0   60
Blood Relics   61
Valentine   63
Night in the Arms of the Two-Hearted Lover   65
Bone Woman   67
La belle au bois dormant   68
Magnetic Declination   69
Battle Lines   70
Santa Muerte   72
Go, Roam   73
A Painting of the Body   75
Contact Prints   77
Things a Girl Should Know   78
Prayer for Protection   79
These Dark Centuries   80
Here, the heart   82
Notes from the Pierce County Sheriff's Department   84
Details   85

Notes   87
Acknowledgments   89

MISSING

The Abduction Narrative

(Girly Chew Hossencofft, 36, missing since September 9, 1999, from Albuquerque, New Mexico)

1. Capture

On the drive home, she still finds bits of glass incandescent in the stillness of the car. Wind scuttling through a hole in her window, symmetrical like a fist. Again, surrounded by the grey light of her room, she leaves an offering to the goddess of mercy poured from the tap. From behind she cannot see the approach of the other woman whose skin phosphoresces with the waning day. And soon, like some tentacled creature, the woman is everywhere, pulling.

2. Procedure

She once helped a boy create a spaceship from cardboard and duct tape. Smoothed ridges over angles. A thing of industry, now looped around her wrists, pulled tight across lips. It is like this that they examine her body. Leave their mark.

3. Tour

Within a triangle, things are lost. There is a house on the moon where he once told her he has been alive for several thousand years, yet still there was strength in his hands the time he wrapped them around her throat. There is a house where he made love to his creature, her skin glittering under arcs of light. And there is her home, the fiery orange carpet creased with bleach and the goddess of mercy keeping watch.

4. Time

On the road to Magdalena, sound is cyclical. This is how minutes go missing. There is just breathing. The dry sound of gestures. Voices. It is easy to forget what came before: the scent of jackfruit and fig, the weight of air before a monsoon, the electric blue heat that used to be love.

5. Return

The narrative leaves space for her body's return. A ritual passage from one place to another. The ability to be left with a sense of foreboding. It remains empty.

6. Aftermath

In the distance, like Bengal lights, beams of light flash by on the highways. Incandescent lanes scaling through the sand. Here, the air is cleansed of water. The breeze heavy with iron as the world seems to collapse in on itself. This is the way stars burn out.

Conductance

(Virginia Pictou-Noyes, 26, missing since April 24, 1993, from Bangor, Maine)

The brothers beat love
into her skin under the pulse-electric
hum of the tavern bar sign.

And her body conducts
the static swell of nightair
into the violet bloom of oiled tarmac.

They beat love as blood sparks
across the dark pavement
like small electrodes.

And her body conducts
the cries of children caught in a nightfire
into the stinging bulb of loosened teeth.

They beat love while each man
tells her she is like a hook,
burst deep into their lips.

And her body conducts
the cold yellow moon, nightnicked
into a grid of blood at her wrists.

The brothers beat love into her skin
while the stars die out.

Cynosure

(Mary Shotwell Little, 26, missing since October 14, 1965, from Atlanta, Georgia)

He gives her red roses stripped of thorns, delivered in cellophane that crinkles in her hands while she looks for the note that reads *secret admirer.*

He gives her his body pressing against hers pressing against her car, his hand cupping her mouth, his voice in her ear asking her if she recalls what it felt like when he ran his fingers down her neck.

He gives her a cheek pressed against dim grey upholstery, her groceries rolling around the backseat clashing into her legs, her scarab bracelet callusing her wrist.

He gives her the sparkle of mile markers, a way to count the distance from her husband's hands.

He gives her a green sign that announces her hometown, and because the morning sun scorches the letters, she cannot see the name, but she knows where she is, remembers the curvature of the road, the dips and rises that announce lovers' lanes, the cobbling together of buildings along the skyline.

He gives her the ticking of a streetlight outside a gas station where she gets out to use a restroom while he and an attendant holding a greasy rag watch her stumble in her bare feet, blood twirling around her knees.

He gives her the percussion of rain on her body, the rivulets of water down her collarbone, the float of crisp red leaves against her wrists and across her back, the hush of roadways.

He gives her the joining of body and ground.

Surrender, Dorothy

(Lola Celli, 24, missing since February 23, 1946, from Grandview
Heights, Ohio)

The name of the star
was sorrow, but her tongue caught

no dust, no whirling tumbleweeds
stuck deep in her throat.

What if she didn't want to see
other lands, big mountains, big oceans

except through the glass light beneath
Marvel's hands?

She wouldn't have plucked
an apple from beneath

glimmering leaves while a toucan
watched the way her lips

moved over its flesh,
or caressed the locked jaw

of a man without heart
enough not to yield an ax.

When the hand of God
reached to hold her

own, she wouldn't have fought
with her eyes closed, or slid

off the edge of the screen
into the technicolor spaces

we only see in the poppy-drunk dawn.
She would have left

those ruby red slippers
on the road through the nightmare forest,

evidence that hearts will never be practical,
until they can be made unbreakable.

Dustland Fairytale

(Deanna Michelle Merryfield, 13, missing since July 22, 1990, from Killeen, Texas)

Inside the car she slides against corsages of cigarette smoke and their foxed skin. The one with star-clustered lips kisses her wrist flesh, the blue of veins. She plans a revelation of pierced skin. Holes safety pin deep, rubbed warm with India ink.

They pull through the ruts of the trailer park, the murmur of dust behind them. Door creaking and footsteps the only dark sounds. At her uncle's she traces hearts on her twin's window, two unmirrored halves. Tapping on the glass she spells out, "I miss you," hopes her sister hears the words in her dreams.

She slides back, silvered hairs catching on the seat. In the plum-tinctured night her twin sleeps. And she, in that husk of metal, the sallow burn of vodka in her throat.

Madrigal of the Sierra Nevadas

(Theresa Ann Bier, 16, missing since June 1, 1987, from Fresno,
California)

There's a colonnade
of trees straight to the peak

of Shuteye, but the girl and man take
to where the forest pinches close.

Her feet never leave the bed of moss,
but she still cannot navigate

the liquid green alone
without fear of falling.

The man stops and grabs
a leaf and a single brown hair caught

in a sapling cleft. She remembers
her childhood book, one with a picture

of an ape-like creature teetering
on two legs, his head turned back.

She remembers his face set in sorrow,
the moment before tears stained his dark fur.

Scorpiris

(Iris Brown, 27, missing since March 13, 1976, from Burlington, Vermont. Murdered by William Posey.)

Iris

Posey

Construction

Three sepals will always sink forward into a fall while three rise above the thick stalk, a standard of silence. This small flower, designed for survival, knows the trickery of attraction. Insects coat themselves in pollen on their way through a petaled path and find the next bloom.

of shape, how curvature is akin to the law

Use

These six-lobed flowers planted along river banks capture poisons amongst their thick roots. This is how they save us, petals and root oxidized for five years, crushed into gin.

remedies for cell mutation and the burn of

Goddess

Eiris: messenger. Iris: rainbow. And this
iridescent creature travels the pathways
between the underworld and the heavens
on small golden wings hung from the sharp
turns of her shoulder blades. She fills clouds
for us, pulls seawater from oceans.

and delivers the gift of madness

Woman

Not flower. Not efflorescence. Not daughter
of sea and wind. That morning, with her
cheeks cold-flushed red, she opened the car
door, trusting,

lips pressed hot against

Not mythical creature. Not sweet sedative.
Not rooted blades. That morning, in the
frosted daybreak when she held golden light
in her palm, hoping for a reunion with her
lover.

dark he waited for her until

Not spectrum of light. Not heart-struck violet.
Not crushed petals. That morning, with her
hand clutched against door handle, she
realized it was all a ruse.

That morning, on a deserted stretch of
highway, there was no movement after he
wrapped his fingers around her throat.

face pushed away from his and her

Not sweet powdered cocaine cut with sugar.
Not stolen moment. Not belief in breath. But
this:

Backland

(Bessie Ann Kutnak, 63, missing since August 16, 1992, from Cameron, Texas)

The grazier tamps down
grass. Work-boots rub
against verdisgrised skin.

Behind her, the murk
of the farmhouse. Still
with rain, huddled
along the hillcrest.

Ahead, the horizon,
an opaline emulsion
of air and ground,
the coming night.

She barely notes the spice
in the air, or planetary revolutions
of aphids in the sharp grass.
They rotate around foxtails,
bent on the collision of selves,
the tangling of bodies.

She wades forward.
Listens for lulling bellows,
the stagger of hooves.
She thinks she sees a dart
of black against the ground.

Closer, against her eye,
a sliver of shadow. Dark,
until her fingers feel like the calving
of ice.

Bloom

(Ann Miller, 21; Renee Bruhl, 19; Patricia Blough, 19; missing since July 2, 1966, from Indiana Dunes State Park, Chesterton, Indiana)

1.

Forty-seven miles of city then open road then lake. She drives with both hands on the wheel, head cocked to the side to take in all the laughter. Like heliotropic flowers, they follow the sun. Faces flushed and filaments of hair twisting in the wind, tangling on lips waxed with cherry lip balm. She dangles her hand outside and at sixty miles an hour catches the air in her palm. At the beach, she slides down a barchan dune, the world giving way beneath her. She feels the burn of the sand. The heat of every granule. She shimmies out of her shorts as though every man is watching, as though every man can see the curve of her belly, the swelling in her breasts. Splaying her fingers around her navel she frames a square. Beneath her fingers the world rests inside, body curled end to end.

2.

She sifts quartz and garnet through her fingers. Pushes down until the sand pushes back. She wishes the earth was less resistant, would let her sink down. Cradle her in silence. In a place where her husband isn't, where his voice can't reach. Topside it's all noise, children sluicing through the sand, women flipping the pages of magazines, water lazing its way forward and back. She silences the hum in her ribcage with normalcy. Smile. Laugh. Smooth on sunscreen. These are all ways to escape the clawing in her throat. She adjusts her purse. Moves it close, but then it is too close. Moves it further away, but it seems out of reach. Inside, the letter she'll never send, the one that would ease the pain from her limbs.

3.

In another country, her horse races against the pull of dirt. A sure thing, they say, though she'll never know. For her the fight is water. When it purls around her hips, she founders. Thrashes her hands out.

Nearby her friends ride out the small waves, sling their bodies forward and let the water cinch them around their waists. They wade out so far that soon she is drifting them toward the boat. With every step plants grasp her ankles. She casts herself toward metal, plastic, veneered wood. The last to get on board. The man's fingers wrap around her wrist, press deep into the knob of bone there. The boat is white, its inside turquoise like a half-opened shell. Running her fingers through her hair, the ends dampened by that seething thing below them, the girl smiles. She joins her friends on the fold-out seats and stretches her legs before her. Absorbs the sun. Soon, her skin will bloom red.

In the Midst of a Divorce

(Nahida Ahmed Khatib, 30, missing since October 1, 1976, from
Wauwatosa, Wisconsin)

Fishermen find a skull
in the Menomonee River

one April afternoon
thirty years after you left

your niece alone
in your sister's house,

frozen meat slabbed
to the counter, a half-empty

coffee cup ringing
the hard surface.

There are men who carry
you all of these years,

the dark wings
of your hair, the scars

marking your body.
A single portrait

of you smiling, tucked
into their shirt pockets.

That skull, not yours,
but that husband

once was, the one
who says you left

in the first place.

What the Eye Can't See

(Promila Mehta-Paul, 70, missing since March 21, 2011, from Munster, Indiana)

The human eye can recover
from injury
in days.

But the way her son's hands
feel marking
her body

is as much her surrender
as when he was inside
her body.

There is no way to recover
from this, or understand
why the human eye

cannot see the colors
of a passing car
in the dark

without the moon to light
the landscape below
in slivers.

Though she sees the way to light
the pathways across
her son's palm

everything is already dying
and living out here
in the dark.

Ornithology

(Lilawattie Buerattan, 35, missing since June 2, 1994, from Loxahatchee, Florida)

Hyacinth Macaw
They carve nests into the flesh of trees,
widen cavities to make way for thick-feathered bodies.

Sometimes they lay two eggs, but only the first to hatch lives.
But this is the way of survival, insurance against the darkness.

To capture a hyacinth macaw, cut down the tree it lives in,
and when that hard-won nesting ground falls

to the forest floor, grab hold and hope to escape
the curved beak and mark of its scaled tongue.

These are the birds she collects inside cages,
the damp heat of the wetlands welcoming them home.

Hawk-headed Parrot
It is said parrots learn to speak out of love,
but they don't know the language of the human heart.

In the high rooms of London, Casanova taught his parrot
how to call his former lover a whore,

another word for his misplaced affections. He forgot
the birds know how to bring the curse of bad luck,

because the parrots with heads shaped like hawks
do not love. In the forests, they are caught

with fishing line and nets. On boats, they are submerged
in water to ensure silence. The time needed to survive

calculated at each border crossing. At the aviary, most are dead.
Parasitic infection and heat. The starving space of wingspans.

Jardine's Parrot
Through the stridor of song, the molt of feathers,
the birds founder. Fall in toward each other, keels collapsing,

floating bone into bone. There, valleys of down clutch
beaks against chests. Beneath the weight of their moldering bodies,

tiny nests still cradle eggs whose insides harden
in the choleric sun. The fledglings yet to develop

egg teeth suffocate. Inside a toolbox, two small Jardine's parrots
wrapped in fabric, their orange irises frozen.

This is how the dead and living are transported, bodies
unnoticed. During that long summer, strands of her hair,

blown by everglade winds, tuck against the aviaries,
just out of reach of tiny, desperate beaks.

This is what the heart sounds like

(Beverly Sharpman, 17, missing since September 11, 1947, from
Philadelphia, Pennsylvania)

At a speed she doesn't recognize, the train leaves Philadelphia heading
toward Chicago. Once on board she'll know that it leads to someplace
other. She'll have her suitcase tucked against her knees and cash rolled
tight in her pocket. Outside the window, trees will dapple the ground
ebony. Hits of sunlight will drown her vision red like a pricked finger.

Before she leaves, she will try to say what this thing is that drives her to
the station late that morning. In front of a mirror, with her skin pulled
tight over her cheekbones, it will be the sound of the hutsmen that
sends her running. That man with a knife and a promise to bring back
beauty.

She'll love him, the stranger that smelled of forest and the hart he
brought down to fill a lie. Those lies, those simple untruths about
where he's been to hide that he found the quiet girl. On the train she'll
finally know what love makes of us. There will be a shadow lodged in
her chest that stutters in time to the sound of metal on metal.

The Fox Twin Theaters Plays *The Omen*

(Cynthia May Hernandez, 20, missing since August 26, 1976, from
Glendora, California)

If something frightening happens today,
it means the earth moves in circles.

On the screen a woman hung
from a window and the bearer of fire
was in the shape of a black dog.
She let popcorn dissolve
in her mouth as a man died
by the cross, as a woman fell
from the stairs.

And the words, "The child is dead,"
echoed through the theater.

Somewhere, swans swim on a river
and a comet fills the sky.
And here, outside the theater,
she walks on a sea of knives.
The night thorn dark,
heavy with the sound of leaves.

Here is our hope: the star of Bethlehem
will destroy all the sons of tumult.

You are one day closer.

Light/Dark

(Shelly Kathleen Sikes, 19, missing since May 24, 1986, from Galveston, Texas)

Carving through the violet night, the men see shadows of the dead hiding in the cypress trees. The shadow-men flick their lips and hands under canopies of foliage. They are looking for flesh. The men push the pedal down as the road dissolves into an ocean of smoke.

Ahead, a girl is driving home, keeping the wheels tight to the yellow line. She reaches her hand out the window, stretches toward the ravished stars. She holds one on the tip of her finger. It doesn't burn. The girl is too busy to notice the headlights flashing off the sky, the trees, her own body. When the car hits her own it feels less like an impact and more like an unfurling.

While the men crack her open, stretch her out, she thinks of the shells on the beach near Galveston. How she followed them in her bare feet after work because they seemed like a path to a place other than one that pumps black into the sky. When the men pull her into the mud, she doesn't mind that her palms collect damp velvet and that her knees are splayed in the dark.

In a field, the girl still takes in the salty dark as the men cut open the earth. Near her left eye are bristled tufts of grass. In the distance, fireflies setting themselves on fire.

Rubicon

(Sharon Baldeagle, 12, missing since September 18, 1984, from Eagle Butte, South Dakota)

Just past home, the dawn flames
across paintbrush until the prairie
bursts into red.

They left Eagle Butte a lifetime ago
and became small nymphs, hips cocked
to the side, thumbs flung out
with abandon.

The highway to oil city flushes
with moisture and the blistering glint
of side-view mirrors, so when the truck
pulls to the side it is a moment
of luck.

Inside his house the man offers
$100 for services rendered,
and they notice a horseshoe hung
above a doorway, meant to collect
good fortune along
its iron rim.

In school they learned lines
of arithmetic, the history
of colonization, but never learned
the way to escape
plastic rope.

The oldest snarls herself
loose, and there's a breath
when it seems the two
will remain.

But the room condenses
until it is a space holding
just one.

The Body in Motion

(Jean Spangler, 27, missing since October 7, 1949, from Los Angeles,
California)

I.

In the dance numbers, it is all lighting and feathers. That's how they
trick the eye. The girls have yet to hit puberty, their hips just bone, their
hair baby-soft. Under hot overheads, they hit their marks in the chorus
line over and over. Kicks high, heads tilted, smiles pasted cutouts.
Their dreams are spangled things. In the books, they are just numbers,
height and weight duly recorded, but on stage, with their feet clipping
against the boards, they are spiritual beings. The vibration of matter in
air.

II.

In the back room clouded with face powder, the woman with Snow
White looks has stopped telling her age or that she birthed a daughter,
holds another inside of her. She keeps moving, embodies change.
Walking the streets, she mirrors those in front of her, constructs a
shadow dance of limbs and torso twists. The choreography is always
new. But on her way to remove part of herself, she falls into her own
steps. In her greatest act, she performs the dance of grieving. She
becomes a maenad.

The Origin of Language

(Sequoya Vargas, 16, missing since August 22, 1993, from Hilo, Hawaii)

The fall into Pele's arms
is not gentle,
nor is the half-struck
dark and passage
of headlights
over skin.

An ironwood tree
rustles. Alone,
it could be mistaken
for the ocean.

She wants
to bridge her body
close to the fractured
bark, hold back the sea
cliff and stare
of moonlight.

She does not know
how one thing leads
to the next. How the wet rot
of vegetation on the shore
road becomes
heady rye of alcohol.
How her body leaves soil
for air and water.

But like all things,
it can be reduced
to a beginning.
Not the moment

she opened
the door or slid
a chess piece across
a board. It begins
in the place they do,
in the murk
where three boys
began to take breath.

She once believed
a conch shell held
to the ear
sounds like the ocean.
When they said
it was a reflection
of pulse, a trickery
of the inner ear,
she believed
they didn't speak
the language.

But here
is where she learns
this beat of light
and salt sounds nothing
like the inside
of a shell.

Inamorato

(Dorothy Harriet Camille Arnold, 27, missing since December 12, 1910,
from New York, New York)

What is meant by a blue serge suit
with its buttons neatly fastened,
      the placement of perfume at your wrists,
its scent crushed from petals
and fixed with essence derived from beavers
      whose small deaths are part of the process?
What is meant by your walk along sidewalks
crimsoned with ice, where chocolates are bought
      in a shop whose sugar plums glazed
behind windows pockmarked
with small fingerprints, or your bookstore stop
      where sun-electric dust motes drifted past?
Or what can be said about an earlier secret
weekend, wandering the streets of Baltimore
      with a lover of the quietest sense,
or the post office box swollen
with the tattered envelopes sent
      from abroad nestled against crisp rejections?
Is it the hat that holds the greatest significance,
the one with grey silk roses, or that someone
      showed you how it is done,
slipped off the bow of an ocean liner
into the star-clustered sea?

How the Ocean and the Desert Meet

(Tara Leigh Calico, 19, missing since September 20, 1988, from Belen, New Mexico)

The juggernaut of change paces the girl on the bike. She's caught in the doldrums, her legs pumping and pumping, bringing her farther into the wake of the hulking truck. They pluck her up, net her out of existence. Inside, it's hooks and rope and men. The smell of their bodies, something like creosote and sweat, coats every breathable space. No one explains. With her mouth taped shut, she talks to herself, speaks the lesson of a fairy tale: a trail made with music. A cassette, its words melting. The player's plastic snapping. When there is nothing left, there is no way of following her into the desert.

No one notices when they join a convoy. Everyone heading somewhere fast. The only noise through the window is tires against pavement. Out there it is a wasteland, blanched white by the sun, the sand winnowed into waves. She wants to lie in it. She wants to return her body to salt.

Stridulation

(Cynthia and Jackie Leslie, 15 and 13, missing since July 31, 1974, from Mesa, Arizona)

That claustrophobic night the trees in the orange grove hunched like sleeping flamingos while the sisters two-step shuffled down the block, toeing up dust. They left behind the rows of tin can homes just as the sky pinked, moved away from the echo of every television set playing the same evening news show and the scuttle of scorpions hiding in palm trees that only ever gave thin columns of shade. Their father, body blackening, sat in an armchair as the chemicals took hold in his blood. They told him babysitting, fingers crossed behind backs. On the way to the party, the youngest bumped her sister with her hip, sharp bone clacking against sharp bone. They giggled, thought about the cool press of glass, the taste of malt coating their tongues, the feel of boys' hands sliding up the seams of their jeans, and the rustle of dry lips knotting together.

From behind, a car, its color grit, its engine flattened by the rasp of cicadas pulsing the night air, their hollowed bodies clicking open and closed. The sisters walked on until the headlights burned against their bare skin, but before anything could happen, the girls reached down, grabbed each other's hands and held on tight.

After the Maison de Mere

(Keiosha Felix, 15, missing since April 30, 2012, from Duson, Louisiana)

In the house of mothers, the girls measure
their stretch marks by the widths of their hands,

the thickness of their fingers. We bear the marks
of tigers, they say, palming the fierce sleekness of ripped skin.

But when the girl named Red kissed her baby
she thought nothing of the rippling musculature

of jungle cats, only the way her child's body
thrust against her, the way men thrust their bodies

against her, the way the air and the heat
and the light thrust against her.

This is what they make of us, she tells her daughter,
this is what we make of ourselves. Because what are the words

to say you do not want the rasp of their lips
or the coarseness of their thighs?

And then, she is gone and we are still here
screaming under the star-split sky.

The Reading of the Fates of Love and Death

(Sophia Felicita Moreno, 16, missing since May 11, 1979, from Bryan, Texas)

At the washateria, the mother, the prophetess of all things, foretells the trials of each cousin. With her skirts tucked up around her knees, a folded *Penny Saver* whiskering damp air toward her face, she records fates. She notes fluid around the ankles for a hard pregnancy, sweetness of the breath for illness, or death. She knows which of the girls will sneak out of their windows at night to embrace dark shadows of men whose facial hair will rasp their cheeks. She says she knows all because she notices all. The daughter tucks her fingers up against salted palms, her love line folding over itself. She doesn't want her mother to notice the raw flesh. The night before she'd tried chiles rellenos, burnt them until the pepper skins puckered and darkened. She snatched them out with bare hands, not yet knowing the lesson of caution. She won't tell her mother this, or the way her husband's skin ashes around his elbows, how it scales around his knees. Won't tell her mother how her husband slinks up her body at night, moves her nightgown up around her hips. Instead, she listens to the deep thrum of the machinery and the clink of a zipper against the metal drum.

Rest Your Head Beside the Mountains

(Brianna Maitland, 17, missing since March 19, 2004, from
Montgomery, Vermont)

If you sketched that early morning,
a study of swallow-down and dishwater

would appear before the overpainted
car came into focus. Headlights turned

out, bumper settled into the side
of a wretched farmhouse, both abandoned

like corn husks beside a Vermont road.
Water bottles scattered in the yellowing

grass in the snow-edged clearing
where no footprints leave trace of passage.

Take her sky-grey night layered with fog
and place your head beneath the curtain

where you will see the current that pulls
you here from the backroom of an inn closed

in the years since she's been gone. She never felt
the mountains rising in the distance, watching over

a place where does skim past, a place
where her body was not laid to rest in hollow dirt.

But you will know to leave this haunted place.
You've got to move on.

The Saints of the Last Days

Patron Saint of Girls
(Ann Marie Burr, 8, missing since August 31, 1961, from Tacoma,
Washington)

Pray for this lightning-bright night
to never end. For the rain to always scatter
droplets over those streets, blackened like the pelt

of an animal. Pray for the girls inside
the small house to sleep through the darkness,
close their eyes against dreams and the barking

dogs. Only blind men would circle
around lambs like these whose bodies, shorn
and bared beneath ivory counterpanes,

don't yet know the way women are held
together like a bundle of wood before they are lit
on fire or how to soak up each other's blood

with white cloths. Pray for them not to cross
over the meridian of the window frame. Keep them
inside their beds with chins tucked over hands

unmarked by passage. Keep them from leaving
everything behind in those rooms,
including a single red thread caught on a sliver.

Patron Saint against Wounds
(Rita Jolly, 17, missing since June 29, 1973, from West Linn, Oregon)

Pray that on this evenfall, bees will fly thick
from her mouth. That the honeyed sweetness
of breath moving past her lips is the only wound

the closing of the day needs to muster past.
On this evening as she soldiers
by sidewalks filled with cracks

and dark thistles prickling the edges
of lawns, pray that men will know hearts
are living things, that injuries

can heal if they are cared for. Pray
that the droning vibrations that echo
through the inky shadows are simply

those bees that have gathered too close
to the ivory roses whose stems can be shaped
into crowns. Pray this is the only sound as she falters

along the roadway, her body moving toward sunset,
and that the livid bruise of darkness looming
behind her is not what we imagine.

Patron Saint of Seamstresses
(Vicki Lynn Hollar, 24, missing since August 20, 1973, from Eugene, Oregon)

Pray that she is the kind of woman who knows
how to pull a thread through, stitch
a hem closed with straight lines, and cut

an end loose without shifting, so you can offer
your own thimbleful of blood
to place at the feet of our maternal

heroine, the only one who will know
if the dark man watches her as he does her blood
sisters. Know that you offer for her a relic,

a way to carry her through the passageway
to the dusky vein of a car lot. Pray
that her pink-blushed dress stays neat

and clean. That the latch on her car door
always bolts tight against wanderers. That the ivory dawn
awakens her every morning until she is a grandmother.

And know that your prayers will not be enough
for her to overstep this moment, so that she can darn
this evening closed with her sleep.

Patron Saint of Captives
(Donna Gail Manson, 19, missing since March 12, 1974, from Olympia,
Washington)

Pray the wolf who sleeps in a bed of woven vine
twigs does not rise from his winter hibernal,
that if he wakes, thrashing toward her in the timber-dark,

hex marks are enough to keep him from her
scent. Pray that she will shiver
in the breeze of his passing, that she will feel

his hunting breath through her heart's arteries.
But first, let her enjoy the music of that night, playing
through her ivory skin, transmuting her existence

from a tawny-haired girl into electric current,
ions traveling along arcs as sharp as the moon.
Offer for her pieces of your body

that no quicklime can corrupt. Give to her
words that feel like a knife in her mouth,
a tongue that can set those night hemlocks on fire.

Pray that she will see the summer's first luna
moth light on her window, its legs hooked hard
as a switch in the screen, its scales shining bright as bone.

Patron Saint of Betrayed Victims
(Georgann Hawkins, 18, missing since June 11, 1974, from Seattle,
Washington)

Pray that when she screams in that alley,
those who hear her voice will not settle
deeper into their own sleep. When she walks

past rhododendrons dark as wildfire, heads
heavier than their stems can hold, pray
she will not take the bait of a man

holding a briefcase. This neophyte
does not know the Spanish word for betrayer
or the way the acrid sent of his hands

can be conjugated into welts. Instead, let her make chains
of asters to crown her head, wrap around
the long brown hair he always yearns to touch.

Pray that he will not stifle the wilderness
that rests beneath her breastbone, the ivory
halo that should never be hardened.

But you must know to also bless those whose hearts
will become bitter without her nimble hands touching
their own. Bless those bitter, bitter hearts.

Patron Saint of Orchards
(Nancy Wilcox, 17, missing since October 2, 1974, from Holladay, Utah)

Pray that the orchard stripped bare of fruit
does not cloak her body in its hollows,
that her limbs are not rooted in its undergrove.

Stay her from his cunning tongue,
the one that would hiss along her ivory neck,
and sheathe itself in the sockets of her limbs.

Let her rise from the ground, leaves collected
in her long russet hair, the musk
of fermented fruit nestled against her skin.

Have her collect her clothes from the altars
beneath the trees and bless the passing
insects as she orients herself in the gloaming.

Pray that the marrow does not leech
from her bones or that her pelvic
arch does not settle into dirt so many miles

from home. Pray that she does not feel his hands
settling along the curve of her neck
or the radial beats of her body fluttering silent.

Patron Saint of Never Failing Hope
(Debra Kent, 17, missing since November 8, 1974, from Bountiful, Utah)

Pray there is enough starlight to ignite
the darkness and turn luminous strands
of her hair as she walks to her car. Pray

there is enough light shimmering on the surface
of the parking lot that he is kept at bay,
not pure enough to enter the space where galaxies

take shape. Pray that our stargazer
will always take this worn stage, stretch
her limbs across windblown distances on the way

to somewhere other than here. Bless her
every time she becomes someone else, places a mask
over her face, but pray she does not learn this from him.

Know that on this night there is another girl locked
into his handcuffs, bruises mottling her wrists.
She, the parallel to ours. Pray there is enough

in this world for them both to greet a new morning,
enough for both of them to turn off the porch lights,
leaving nothing to gather insects in ivory cups.

Patron Saint of Travelers in the Mountains
(Julie Cunningham, 26, missing since March 15, 1975, from Vail,
Colorado)

Pray that the snow will become blinding
enough to hide her from view as she darts
from the tavern on her way home.

Let the wind savage her small frame and gather damp
ivory flakes into the crook of her neck. Let it pitch
her body into a strand of moss-dark trees.

Anything, pray for anything to keep her
from the man on crutches, his lips cocked
in an apologetic smile. Pray the wind takes her

and spits her out on the other side of the mountains,
far from his cuffs and hands and the shovels
he uses to bury them in the night-swollen ground.

But if he finds her, give her prayers that will offer hope.
Pray that she will turn into something feral,
something that will survive the dropping mercury

and the lame man who would scarab her skin with heated breath.
Let her peel the flesh from his bones. Let her be the one
to bury him in the ground again and again.

Patron Saint against Sudden Death
(Denise Lynn Oliverson, 24, missing since April 6, 1975, from Grand
Junction, Colorado)

Pray that the wheels of her bicycle will always turn
over, and the locust-clicking of the chain
will continue propelling her out over city streets.

Pray that she hears the train as she passes,
its steel core thrumming over the trestle, and the viaduct
below full only of her body and the flashing

yellow of her bike. Let the ivory rims quarter
the dampness of the underpass with scattered
light. Pray that he does not come to hold her hand

or cannon his ragged exclamations
into her long, brown hair. If he tries to take
her, pray that she becomes a pillar of stone,

her bones too heavy to move, her wounds
silver veins of magnetite. But, don't pray for her
to be locked safe in a tower, her body fed

with nectar and her skin scented with oils. Don't pray
for her hair to grow long enough to climb, or for a man
to pursue her as she flees. Pray instead for revolution.

Patron Saint of Drowning Victims
(Lynette Culver, 12, missing since May 6, 1975, from Pocatello, Idaho)

Pray that when the water comes for her, she reaches
past the break-point. That she does not falter as she holds
her breath deep in her frigid lungs, lungs love-sick

for the touch of air. Pray that the overhead light
in the hotel bathroom flickers like a snake's tongue
tasting the eager night while she keeps her eyes open.

It is not for us to know why a god would take her
to this room, dressed still in her red checkered shirt
and blue jeans. It is not for us to know, but pray

we learn. Pray that we see her rise from the ivory depths
of that bathtub, water sluicing from her skin, the folds
of her body forming it into estuaries, forks branching into arms

big enough to embrace a paramour in their depths.
Pray that it is he who plunges down as far
as the murky porcelain will allow.

Let the light fang over his prone form. Let the chambers
of his heart shutter close. Let the luckless be the one to taste
the mournful keening of his submerged body.

Patron Saint of the Forgotten
(Susan Curtis, 15, missing since June 27, 1975, from Provo, Utah)

Pray that her pulse quickens deep
in her chest, sets her skin trembling
like firefly light. Pray she is able to brace herself

against his foul lips, the kisses he longs
to burn along her cheek. Pray her yellow evening
gown learns to hold the color of the ivory moon

in its angled depths, that it never pools around her ankles,
silent as an afterthought. Bless her for the strength
in her legs, those hardened muscles that carried her

along the fifty miles of highway to this place
of teenagers, to this place of prayers
and offerings. Pray that these legs are strong

enough to make her the one who is faster.
Let her be the one to survive, let her be the one to spin
her body through the divide, past the bone-burning heat

of desert sands, the sharp wrench
of mountains. Send her far enough that his hands cannot reach
the path he would take along her collarbone and neck.

Patron Saint of Martyrs
(Nancy Baird, 23, missing since July 4, 1975, from East Layton, Utah)

Pray that if he arrives at that lonely gas station he finds her
armed with a sword that will spread his blood
across the ground like rubies. Pray

that she is ready to usher him toward his last
breath. But if she's not, pray that women
will never go to bed dreaming of the taste

of his skin across their tongues. Let them know he would
poison them, strip them of heartbeats
and the feeling of morning air, ivory-sharp against their faces.

Let them know if he could, he would wrap his fingers in their hair
and yank until the crack of their necks is the only sound
to split those endless nights. Pray that we care enough

about our own survival. Pray she doesn't back down
or that we rise with her. Pray that together we tear
this world apart, light him on fire in one sharp electrical burst.

Pray that this life is something we need not fear, that desolate
roads and backwater stations are our haven. That the darkness
of night is our cloak. Pray we do not become martyrs.

UNIDENTIFIED

In the cursed country

(unidentified woman discovered December 2, 1990, in McDonald
County, Missouri)

Who we are is not tethered
cords, or the way our skin
reflects winter light.

We are grace, because memory
is a parachute that falls
quickly until it lights
with a flamed match.

Grace, in that the fox knows
the way to worry bone,
breaking it open
to the soft marrow.

Grace, in land that remembers
it needs to yield
to coming frost,
that preserver of death.

Grace, in a woman
who never forgets
how to carry the weight
of another human
home again.

Detroit, and Other Sorrows

(unidentified woman discovered June 7, 2010, in Detroit, Michigan)

Scrappers abandon
this house, no copper
shine left beneath these walls.

Inside, nails laid against
a bare mattress of cotton
ticking, roach-dark with blood.

This is how women
go missing, bodies acclimated
to the force of wills beyond our own,

Left in the night
when the ghost city's streets go dark,
past houses that used to hold our laughter.

This skeleton house
grips tight to street edges,
where brush gets tangled in our leavings.

It is all that is left
in the dusk as our world contracts,
pulls back on itself like a wounded thing.

There is no cure
for how you abandon this city,
its body stretching for miles past reckoning.

But we know how
to set it on fire, skin it down
to nothing but muscle and bone.

We are Detroit,
and this is what we do.

The Killing Field

(unidentified woman discovered February 2, 1986, Calder Road, League City, Texas)
(unidentified woman discovered September 8, 1991, Calder Road, League City, Texas)

I once held a raw oyster in my mouth, its three-chambered heart fluttering against my tongue. *My tongue once knew a thousand words, the shape of sound.* That night, before he plucked me from the sidewalk, I walked from the payphone, extra change slinking around my pockets. *That night was magnolias, the air hemmed in by their scent.* In the back of his van I counted the ways out, the number of doors, the number of windows, all closed to me. *The windows held the world, that other place.* I scraped my knees, bled into the ground there in the lot. *The lot was earth and oil, tin cans and rope.* The heat of his body refracted off my skin, skimmed the trees in half-darkness. *My skin a mirror, reflecting moonlight and the sucked light of the stars.* Still beneath a tree, my hands folded into a cross, the sign of prayer. *My hands a dove.* There, my body lay fallow. *There, my body lay.*

Our Bodies, the Ocean

(unidentified woman discovered January 23, 2013, in Lattingtown,
New York)

They are looking for women
down at Gilgo Beach, bodies
wound tight with burlap.

Deep in the rushes
they find a man
dressed as a woman,
the small frame
of a child, and women,
so many women
they could form a choir,
these saints of the last days.

It takes more years to find
me, my bones drenched
beneath hurricane
sand and the filmy light
of Oyster Bay. So deep
in this shore I must cast
my body toward fate.

But don't believe there is luck
in wearing a charm for those born
during the Year of the Pig,
the final sign
of those easily fooled
into believing it is anything

other than a way for water to collect
along its curved back
and beneath its golden hooves.

Underbrush

(unidentified woman discovered October 23, 1994, in Sequoyah County, Oklahoma)

Lover mine, there is only silence among the deadfall trees, no space for sound between bone and bark now that you hold the stuttered beating of my heart. The sigh of my lung. And on nights

    of wind and rain

                    we know

        my love for you

            is a fable.

Lover mine, please array my body into the shape of a swan. My arms the smooth swoop of wings to hold this deep October moon. Do not bind the twisted knobs of my ankles, the notches of my wrists. Remember there was once devotion in your touch. When you held

    me in your arms

                  you told me the body

        is meant to be possessed

            which is why I know the architecture

    of your chest,

        that uneven turn

            of your freckles.

Lover mine, find me here again. This cradle of darkness and my body held in state. My chest yearns for its heart, the time it takes for breath. And when we passed

those minutes

with your body

pressed against mine

and the sharp slice

of your knife

oh, how

I grew weary.

Prime

(unidentified woman discovered April 24, 1981, near Troy, Ohio)

The day the Green Man comes,
I wear another life stitched
into a coat. Flayed skin slaps
as he downshifts past,
his eighteen-wheeler humming.
The cab flashes like a lure,
not rotting vegetation or heat
of earth, but cold, hard metal.

Inside, it is hotter than it has a right
to be. Hair spools against the nape
of my neck. With one hand he fingers
a curl, his skin rough like bark.
From the cab, I watch
white lines coursing past.

The Green Man removes
my coat, that piece of flesh.
Turned inside out it's lined
the color of bruising.
He folds it between us,
such a small barrier.

Outside, it is barely spring,
snow still clutching the ground
beneath the thick pine trees.
The Green Man waits for an offering
of blood to bring life.

This I should have remembered.

Fourteen Pounds

(unidentified woman discovered September 30, 1952, near Black Hawk, Colorado)

My soul weighs
no more than twenty-one grams,
a weight that forgets
how it feels to touch one lip
against another,

and the burden of the body
it leaves behind.

And what remains:
the heaviness of blood
spread thin across the gulch.
Dark hair matted
on a stretch of skin.

Charcoaled bone wedged
deep in the scorched earth.
The gasoline burn of the felled
log. The morning dew
sequined on a web
of gristle.

Did you know a magpie's heart
weighs 9.3 ounces?
But what does that say
about how its voice sounds
calling across the divide?

Victim #0

(unidentified woman discovered September 5, 1934, in Bratenahl, Ohio)

Kingsbury Run dyed the world yellow every morning. It was in
the steam of the furnaces, the acid that laced the shore. We braced
ourselves against it, created temples of cardboard and tin cans. The hot
press of metal sheltered us from the wailing sky.

Deep in the scar of earth, I searched for treasure. Broken bits of glass
polished into stars. Whole constellations tined to the ground. There,
in that corroded ravine, fish bloated. Rolled on the dirt, waiting for the
hungriest to pluck them up. By evening, those hungry had retreated far
enough into the reeds so that when the man shambled up, it seemed we
were alone. He held out his hand. And I took it.

After, they'd say how the frame of his body turned into a gambrel to
stretch me loosely. He'd scald me, burn me into ciders. Cure my skin.
Commit me to the cold. There in the lake the light changes. It blisters
through the surface and hides angles of intersection. But I'll find them
down in that water.

Blood Relics

(unidentified woman discovered April 28, 1979, in Newark, New Jersey,
and November 1990 in North Camden, New Jersey)

Come to this desperate place
where my bones have been separate
for so long the notched grooves don't

fit. You need
alignment to answer

why your skull is found
beneath the broken
wood of a house where strong men flex

dark muscles beneath
November's worn out sun.

You will find
the call of your body
is not one of desire. Where the splintered

ache in your chest is simply the curl
of a caterpillar taken root

in the hole where your heart once was.
I thought I knew
how a butterfly becomes

something other than a tongue lost
in words, but it is not how wings grow

from flesh; it is how we are reduced
to liquid and whom we might have kissed
under the whispers

of this tree while singing the night
awake.

Valentine

(unidenitified woman discovered February 15, 1991, in Big Coppitt Key, Florida)

I lost time
among the saints,

the lark, the dove,
the sparrow singing

the rush of ocean
against sand.

The men whisper
the blackbird's cry,

an echo against
our blindness.

The lot was cast and then I drew.

We move across
the sky circumference,

the whistle-down bend
of touch-me-nots

on the shoulders
of sand so far distant

from my hand etched
to your pulse.

And fortune said it shoul'd be you.

Those men, with arms
like soldiers,

in another life
they would bring miracles.

Night in the Arms of the Two-Hearted Lover

(unidentified woman discovered March 26, 1986, near San Antonio,
Texas)

—After Beckian Fritz Goldberg

The night is full of wolves, dear,
and the angels are restless.

Here the dark slit of road unravels
east of the San Antonio line,

and my arms are a cavalry of precision
wrapped hard around your waistband.

Between my thighs, your engine vibrates
dusk across the sky of exposed skin,

and I roll my tongue around yours
because this is what you want.

We rest cheeks against the sides of a farmhouse
like a giant beast we once remembered.

Here we pray to the gods of transformation,
hunters with metal and sacrifice,

and you say you know the evil
of magic woven 'round hoed earth.

Beneath your startled hands
you know the pulse of the shadows.

In the distance, the dark pull
of a train heading north across the flats,

and we both wail, thrashing
against the passage.

Here the night wings flit close
to blood spilled out on Texas sand,

and we hold open our palms
because there's still a heart

beating in the night, dear.

Bone Woman

(unidentified woman discovered May 7, 1990, in Rogers, Arkansas)

There once was a woman
who collected pieces of bone.
Slithered on her stomach
across fields and forests, searching.

She placed pieces of my life
in a bag, so many bones, they rattled.
She sprawled across the ground
with me, the earth black
and seething in the spring damp,
shadowing her palms with dirt.

Even on the ground, the collector
could tell the trajectory of the bullet,
one sharp burst through the skull.
This is what it is called, not head
or brain, but skull. A matter of bone.

Inside her cave, the woman threaded
together what she could. She believed
this is how we are not lost, the reunion
of bone to bone. This creation
of story as though akin to resolution.

But there was not enough, never enough,
because beneath this gathering of bone,
we are both made to be women of flesh.

La belle au bois dormant

(unidentified woman discovered August 14, 1977, in Everett, Washington)

Gifts: (1.) An orange Chevy Nova, the means of transmutability. (2.) A single, bright peacock feather, the bearer of immortality. (3.) A blue woven bungee cord, the measure of air.

Spindle: There is no breath in this cockspur wasteland shot through with brambles. Deep in the briar, with sweet juice over pricked skin, I trace the arc of these bitter roots.

Prince: If I knew contours inside the dark lobes of his heart, this moment would want for love.

Awakening: In the forest of thorns I sleep heavy under the humid sky. This the birth of my own true light. How am I to hold it?

Magnetic Declination

(unidentified woman discovered October 7, 1998, in Weatherford, Texas)

The migration of birds
is elemental. Pieces of magnetite
lodged against vessels.

And, as rain hauls
across the sky, the red tower lights
draw them until it is bone
against metal.

Before my skin
was stitched closed, my body
had wings. Now, there is nothing
magnetic to pull

my fingers across
the humid ground.
Loose strands of thread collapsed
against ribs.

My lips and lungs
no longer believe in dawn or feast,
and I navigate my body
across grass, the prick
of needle

through fold of arm,
and as birds fall in death, I find fire,
their feathers a pulse
against cracked skin.

Battle Lines

(unidentified woman discovered March 1, 1992, in Bitter Creek, Wyoming)

I once kissed
the ruby flesh
of a hummingbird
held against
a rest-stop sign

on a day before I left
my body in ice
at the curve
of a prairie road.

In this life
our blood
is where we make
a fist against
anger.

We tattoo roses
to our chests,
memorials to love
and lost fortunes.

What we sell
is ourselves
to the fluttering
of breath,

when the darkness
is a memory of miles
drifting past windows
of light.

We lose markers
to tell us who we are,
where we are from,
because it is everything
that matters.

Out here, our children
are being eaten by wolves.

Do you hear them?

Santa Muerte

(unidentified woman discovered November 4, 2009, near Casa Grande, Arizona)

Lady of the Shadows,
it has come to this: silvered lines
on my back faded, no clouds
to block heat from my skin.

That angry summer I prayed
for love, offered incense
until my sheets were heavy with you.
And when he finally marked my body,
you came in your white cloak,
gold rings rattling on bone fingers.

Your shrine sat in my garden,
tucked between rock
and the fountain clogged
with Palo Verde blossoms
every spring, the time sun licked
the roof of your temple
with light until you were on fire.

I brought you fresh oranges,
tucked coins beneath packets
of cigarettes, inked you
to my skin. You, lady of night,
I watched the stars for you,
stood witness over the seasons.
For this, I prayed for safety.

Niña Santa, after monsoons drag
across sand, brittlebrush will bloom
for you. Harsh and waiting.

Go, Roam

(unidentified woman discovered August 15, 2011, near Glasgow,
Kentucky)

When the Scythians came,
their bodies and mounts laced
with sweat, the plain birds would go silent.
These men, fed from horse-blood,
scalps hanging
from their reins.

And I, in my dawn, heard the whippoorwills' last calls through the
sycamore trees. No jangle of horse-flesh or rye of sweat along this
highway, just the lonely cries of *whip-poor-will* and the snap of a plastic
bag caught in the underbrush.

When the Visigoths came,
those wandering warriors set across
battlefields with swords drawn.
There, in written law,
the *decalvatio*, or separation
of hair, skin, and skull.

And I, delivered to this barren land, know the distance separating
earth and sky. A finger's-length shimmer rising on the road. The
humid breath of semis passing the horizon in one tight, hot fist.

When John Lovewell came,
his frost-hued men at his heels,
the ponds were still with ice
and the bodies of men killed.
Their cured skins returned
for bounty.

And I, with the slice of a knife across the ridge of my brow, have forgotten the taste of snowflakes on my tongue, the whisper of ice on my lips and the worn-out press of boots against snow. Here, it's just the slow drop of blood on blood.

When Bloody Bill Anderson's soldiers came,
their horses pounding through
Missouri and Kansas, the world fell away
in one blue reckoning.
Slapping against the sides
of their desperate creatures, the scalps
of victories.

A Painting of the Body

(unidentified woman discovered May 4, 2004, in Honolulu, Hawaii.
Died April 27, 2013.)

Why worry   about the break
     of morning
     over the ocean
when it is only
        the static hum   of noise.

Or remember a word
that belonged at the birthing
        of my center
when it can be replaced
by a   syllable.

If there is a crowding
     inside my brain
       that leaves a   small hole
for words
to be forgotten,

then my worn   body
    that recalls years of kneeling
        in the sand, now only needs
to know   the movement
of lovegrass in the wind.

If my mind doesn't know that the name
of the park where my body   is found
        means *path to the sea*,
it also won't know   it is a place to leave
        what is not needed.

But in the end,
what matters
is that this space between flesh   and thought is

    still life.

Contact Prints

(unidentified woman discovered August 22, 1968, near Morgantown,
Berks County, Pennsylvania)
(unidentified woman discovered April 18, 1969, in French Creek State
Park, Berks County, Pennsylvania)

We are half-naked   when we run. Soft white leather shoes glossing
over ground. Those men with their mollusked hands and skin burned
hot   with ink let us go. Let us think   we're free. We hear our own
coarse breathing as we shuttlecock   through the forest. Twigs snap
in our hair, earth and gravel grind loose.

And then we feel them. The hot sliver   of their breath, the rush of
bodies against air. There's no time to scream. We run. We run past
leaves. Past picnic tables. Past the tinny chirrup of birds.

And those men, guns locked in fists, keep pace.

When I let go   of her hand, I feel the hard click of her braceleted
wrist against my own. I don't wait to see her fall. I run   until my
lungs smolder, my knees crack against buried roots. I run until I stop.

Alone through the spring I learn to emulsify. I teach

the stone the contours

of my shoulder,

the line

of my hip.

Things a Girl Should Know

(unidentified woman discovered July 21, 1980, in Eklutna, Alaska)
—*After Tarfia Faizullah*

Remember
        to keep your eyes open when you dance
        naked against a pole; the customers want
to pretend
        you move your body for them. Remember
        to buy heels so tall and sharp
they are daggers
        you can use to run down a man's body, catching
        against rib bones on the way. When you buy new clothing
it doesn't matter
        how short or tight, as long as you take
        it off. When a man wants to photograph you, ask him, ask him
if he's ever killed
        before. He will say no, but listen for the ratchet of breath
        in his chest, the way his pupils dilate under the club lights.
If he tells you
        to run, you will never be fast enough to escape
        the sight of his gun, the sharp tug of his knife.
He will bring you
        to the wilderness, the place where the ice crusts thick, to hunt
        you among the scrub. If you have sold your body to dance, or
the touch
        of someone's skin on yours, then when he parts your slit
        flesh, some will say this is your fault. But listen for the sound
of the river
        changing direction. This is the moment
        you hold your breath.

Prayer for Protection

(unidentified woman discovered December 9, 1990, on the bank of the Passaic River, North Arlington, New Jersey)

We are born with the mark of the devil, bathed in darkness. Here and here fire scarred across my skin, the lick of his tongue. My grandmother, the same burned heat wrapped around her crisp ankle. She held sugar in her hands the night he came. Specks of cane candying her arms. He found her on the road as she heaved under the press of smoke. Wrapping his fingers around the cleft of her chin, he pulled her down in the burnt field.

He comes to my bed. Tries to crawl in through my nose, ears, eyes. My grandmother smells his sulfurous kiss in my hair. Piercing the meat of a garlic clove with her sewing needle, she makes a necklace held with red thread.

Now by the cold river, his cloven hooves etch the ground with desire. Gathered in my hand, the mud seems too small to hold the weight of sin. When he comes, he will hold the world. We will embrace in the grip of water. He will be handsome. He will be the ragged goat. He will be my heart.

These Dark Centuries

(unidentified woman discovered March 21, 1984, in Seattle,
    Washington)

The city night burns out
under electricity while the man
holds a blurry photograph.
He says, *This is my son. This is the boy I lost.*
They don't give you anything
out here, but it could be true.
Down the street is a singed-out field,
a hard diamond etched in the ground.
I would take my boy there to play, he says.
If only I had the chance.

(unidentified woman discovered August 21, 2003, in Kent, Washington)

From here, the Green River reeks
of mud and rot. The truck, salt-slicked
and sexed. The door opens.
I shift pieces of myself back
before clattering to the concrete.
There are two of us in this dark dance.
Goodbye, he whispers against
my hair as he cinches an arm
around my throat. It is connective,
this drawing of breath and night.

(unidentified woman discovered February 18, 1984, in Federal Way,
    Washington, and January 2, 1986 in Auburn, Washington)

The city night ends,
becomes grey. Overhead, the shrill
seagulls, the hot trail

of airplanes. Beyond, the rising
traffic, the reckoning of names
on granite markers. This is the edge
of land, the hard note of dawn
tugging at this horizon,

where an ecstasy of form
is defined as body.

Here, the heart

(unidentified women discovered between 1934 and 2008 in the United States)

To grow hearts
inside a laboratory,
you have to care enough
to keep them alive.

remains

> beneath a bridge: burlap, newspaper, skeleton, an advertisement for the theater. The company sent a letter proposing disappearance and the girls performed, playing the missing.

Scientists sleep
beside glass houses
every night and wake
at dawn to begin again.

remains

> discovered near an underpass. Rural death near mile post 23. Examination revealed height, weights, approximate age. A charm of death.

Inside, cells
divide, take shape
along a predestined
plan. The hearts know

remains

> in Cranbury Township. Pierced blue and outline of bone. Birth month of March and a twisted horseshoe strap.

their worth. What we mean
by life, is something small
and necessary. A force
greater than its sum,

remains

> spotted by a fisherman between Lake Lavon and Lake Ray Hubbard. She was awakened from sleep.

how one thing transforms
into something else.
In other laboratories,
the scientists grow

remains

> near a track, wrapped in red and the knife marks there to trace.

miniature versions,
hearts smaller
than a kiss. They inject
chemicals to enlarge

remains

> with a tattoo of a peach in the shape of a heart.

the cells. Introduce disease
where there was none
so they can watch
the hearts expand,

grow past the boundaries
of what they were made for.
And this is how,
in that light,

remains

pulled from the woods along Canal Road by
a man hunting scattered bones.

remains

are a torso and two legs washed ashore
two days apart. Cold on the beach, a storm
floods blue. And, when pieced together, the
phrase, "begin to live."

remains

in a vacant lot. Her heart surrounded by
blackberry bushes.

a heart begins to die.

Notes from the Pierce County Sheriff's Department

(unidentified woman discovered December 11, 1976, in McKenna, Pierce County, Washington)
(unidentified woman discovered August 29, 1978, in Elbe, Pierce County, Washington)

We forgot the beat of memory, the way we once leaned back on Tilt-a-Whirls, hair trailing on the ground as the greening world collapsed into one long constellation of light,

how the terror-ache of desire seemed to slip free from skin.

We forgot what we once asked of your bodies: tell us how your bristled length spiraled in water, how deep the thickets on the side of a mountain are in summer,

how the dust of planetary objects can feel like love.

We forgot the way our hearts are strung to yours, the jungle-heated touch of our hands on your hands so that we no longer knew

how the body can be land-filled, knobs of vertebrae and the firethorn sharp curve of rib.

We forgot

how we lost you.

Details

(unidentified woman discovered June 14, 1995, in Lassen County,
California)

She had good teeth.

Notes

"Surrender, Dorothy" contains lines from L. Frank Baum's *The Wonderful Wizard of Oz.*

"Dustland Fairytale": This title is taken from a song by The Killers.

"In the cursed country": This title is taken from a line by Joy Harjo.

"Detroit, and Other Sorrows": The last two lines of the poem are the tagline for the city of Detroit.

"Valentine" contains lines from *Gammar Gurton's Garland* by Joseph Ritson.

Acknowledgments

Poems from this manuscript have appeared in, sometimes in slightly different forms, the following publications:

The Adroit Journal: The Fox Twin Theaters Plays *The Omen*
Barn Owl Review: Light/Dark
Bat City Review: Contact Prints
Copper Nickel: Cynosure; The Reading of the Fates of Love and Death; Stridulation
The Florida Review: The Body in Motion
Fourteen Hills: Bloom
Guernica: The Saints of the Last Days
Harpur Palate: Battle Lines; Fourteen Pounds
The Heart is Improvisational: an Anthology in Poetic Form: Night in the Arms of the Two-Hearted Lover
The Journal: Things a Girl Should Know
The Massachusetts Review: The Abduction Narrative
Natural Bridge: The Killing Field
The Pinch: Night in the Arms of the Two-Hearted Lover; Underbrush
Puerto del Sol: A Painting of the Body
Quarterly West: Backland; Detroit, and Other Sorrows; Madrigal of the Sierra Nevadas; Scorpiris
Quiddity: Our Bodies, the Ocean; Prime
Sonora Review: These Dark Centuries
The Southern Review: How the Ocean and the Desert Meet; Prayer for Protection; This is what the heart sounds like; Victim #0
Stone Canoe: Dustland Fairytale
Thrush: In the cursed country; Notes from the Pierce County Sheriff's Department; Santa Muerte
Washington Square Review: Blood Relics
Witness: Go, Roam

Aimée Baker is a multi-genre writer with work appearing in *The Southern Review*, *Gulf Coast*, *Guernica*, *The Massachusetts Review*, and others. In 2014, she was awarded the Zoland Poetry Fellowship from the Vermont Studio Center. Baker received her MFA from Arizona State University. She currently lives in upstate New York with her husband and daughter and teaches as a lecturer at SUNY Plattsburgh, where she also serves as fiction editor for *Saranac Review*.